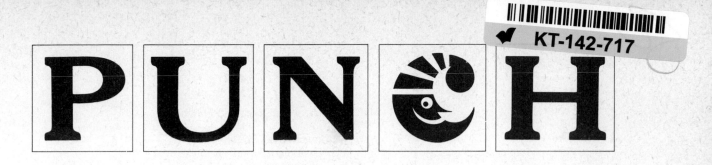

PUNCH

The Battle of the Sexes

First published in Great Britain in 1984 by

Octopus Books Limited
59 Grosvenor Street
London W1

ISBN 0 86273 167 4

Made and printed in Great Britain by
Richard Clay (The Chaucer Press) Limited
Bungay, Suffolk

"... Only 6,000 miles on the clock. The front's all crumpled, the paintwork's in a mess ..."

"*I'm not bothered; Elwood is always faithful to me. In his fashion, of course.*"

"*Sorry J. B., there's been a takeover bid.*"

"*Why don't I go and slip into a skirt?*"

"Look, if you're a single parent, perhaps you'd care to join our ménage à trois."

"He walked out on her, leaving her with three young children and her husband."

"I'm terribly sorry—it's the first time I've ever done this."

"Hello, wall. Did you have a good day today? My big news is I discovered a new, miracle washday product that has me all excited . . ."

"One step nearer and I'll write to 'Guardian Women'!"

"'Three Women in a Boat'—I like it!"

"Go forth and seek the bluebird of happiness and on your way home pick up a loaf of pumpernickel."

"Typical! The file on women is in the very last drawer."

"She still won't confess to causing this bloody drought."

"We've decided against divorce. Neither of us wants custody of the dog."

"I suppose it's the element of danger, but it's the cigarette afterwards that's really terrific!"

"Your accountant will have explained the difference between tax evasion and tax avoidance—well, the same principle applies to birth control."

*"How much brighter and more alive everything seems
with a new carburettor."*

"The sun was shining, the birds were singing while the daffodils were waving gently in the light breeze . . . suddenly the sap began to rise . . ."

"I suppose two can live as cheaply as one providing they both go out to work."

"This is Eastertide, Amos. Christmas
was the season to be jolly."

"You mean that now you've seen me walking, you don't find
me romantic anymore?"

"Ed, I'd like you to meet Sally Dunbar, Frank Cheswicke's No. 1, Owen Liswald's No. 3, Ralph Frandenburgh's No. 2 and now my No. 2."

"He loves flouting the libel laws."

"*She always had to have the last bloody word!*"

"Don't move, lady. There's a water
pistol aimed right at your hair."

"OK, so it won't be a good time,
but it'll take the weight off your
feet for a bit."

"*Grenades, grenades, I know they're in here somewhere.*"

"Steady, love, try to see it as 150 tons of foundation cream."

*"He was leaning on a lamp-post at the
corner of the street until a certain little
lady passed by."*

*"Part of our trouble was that she was AD
and I was BC."*

"I trust, sir, your wife has given you carte blanche to choose the wallpaper?"

"At home is one thing. At the office you must snap out of defeats without feeling shattered."

"It's a fortnight since I came out of the closet
and still nobody's noticed that I'm wearing
my wife's clothes."

"We could have been here yesterday but he had to re-decorate the bedroom!"

"Wilbur and I always tell one another when someone has attracted us, and that tends to nip things in the bud."

"Sexual harassment? Because I admired your notebook?"

"I've just realized—I don't even know your nom de plume."

*"Somebody's Daddy obviously didn't keep
up the maintenance payments."*

"She was terribly attached to Rupert!"

"I too have always been used to sleeping on this side of the bed!"

"Big smile, everybody."

"*I'd like someone who will feel guilty for the rest of her life after I kill myself when she rejects me.*"

"I pretend to be pregnant at least once a year—you get such terrific treatment."

"I didn't realize she was a
career woman."

*"For twenty years I've thought of you as selfish
and boring—now I think of you as J.R."*

*"I expect you're madly attractive
en masse."*

*"Tell her I've had her blood cleaned off the carpet and I've
sent the carving knife in to be re-sharpened."*

"*Frankly, I lost faith in your judgement when you saved our marriage in the first place.*"

"*I'm afraid I must replace you, Miss Thomas—you are releasing in me frustrations and passions which I normally reserve for the business.*"

"I only hope it isn't a replica."

"I was wondering, Miss Prossier, if
you have ever given any
consideration to the idea of making
a complete fool of me . . .?"

"What's happened to us? We never
ask what's happened to us any more."

"Not the old run-out-of-money line!"

"It's only September—why don't I stay the night?"

"Of course you're a failure, who else gets letters from Reader's Digest saying they haven't been selected for the latest prize draw?"

"Can't he play anything else but 'Strangers in the Night'?"

Colin Whittock.

"Oh, he'll come crawling back in a couple of days. He always does."

"Just think, three weeks ago you were only a telephone number among the graffiti."

"Sometimes—just sometimes—I think it would be nice to be the victim of a sexist remark."

"This probably contravenes the Code of Practice but. . ."

"It's the dustman, dear, and I'd run out of money."

"All I can say is you're not the
ex-husband my first
ex-husband was!"

"I would marry you, George, but are you sure we haven't been married before?"

"He'll think of you every time he scores."

"It must be Spring. The divorce petitions are pouring in."

"Backache? Yes, the wife found a hot bath helped hers."

"And to my wife, Helen, I leave our marriage."

". . . and Horace is signalling his delight at your dinner invitation."

"Andrew, you're uneducated. Be so good as to explain this programme to me."

"*His wife's divorcing him—he's probably working out how much she'll claim if he sinks it.*"

"How patronizing do you like your equality?"

"Now that's a typical bloody woman's generalization!"

"Whatever happened to that heart of gold you used to be a tart with?"

"He must have flown to New York
—he had very little money on
him when he left."

"There you go, listening down to me again."

"It's very original of you, Jason—but is a silicon chip for ever?"

"George usually manages to get home for Sunday lunch."

"While you were married to Roger, Igor, Peregrine and Bartley and I was married to Mary-Anne, Elissa, Fay, Bobo and Sophia, I always knew we were meant for each other."

"The mating season was last month."

"Men—you're all the same!"

BANX

"Well, do you want to start off tonight's argument with a real zinger or shall I?"

"Ta Dah-h-h-h! Tonight Jardin Potager is proud to present: You've seen this before and you'll see it again hash."

"*Norman has never been what you might call ambitious.*"

"*All that small print has given me a headache.*"

"You never use emotional blackmail against me any more."

"Pamela, if you'll just have a seat over there, I'll start my mating dance."

"Men! Is that all you ever think about?"

"I can never get him to do a thing at home."

"As a footnote to history, I want it known
that Angelica has been one hell of a good
concubine."

"I love him, and he loves me. But
basically we hate each other."

"Look, if you can't adjust to a new teacher once in a while, how are you going to cope with a second or third marriage?"

"For the first time in your life you're ahead of a trend, dear."

"We have separate bedrooms. I live here and he lives with this
other woman in Clapham."

"This lawn gets worse every year!"

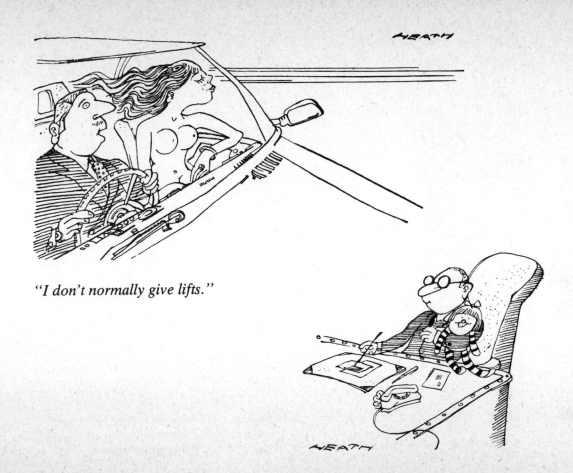

"I don't normally give lifts."

"He claims it's an executive toy."

"I can't help it—I always laugh at weddings."

"How can you wonder which wine to have when the big issue is which of us is going to get the wine-list!"

"*Do you think there will be sexual
harassment after death?*"

"Is there someone else, Gervaise, or do you really go to the Crusades every Thursday?"

"An executive toy? It looks suspiciously like housework to me."

*"You're a man—you must have some idea what I should buy
my husband for Christmas?"*

"It's the librarian calling for you . . .
she's a month overdue."

"I've asked you here because I
want a divorce."

"Just browsing, thank you."

"She feels she can improve on the
time it takes to boil an egg."

"I certainly wouldn't want to go
through that again!"

"That's the trouble with you men, all you want is friendship!"

"He seems to have lost the urge since his accident."

"*Mr and Mrs R. Crawford Richardson announce
with pleasure the break-up of their marriage.*"

"*Before we leave I'll get him to wash the tea cups.*"

"Play something dramatic, Findlay. Miss Swanson and I are having a row!"

"Lack of communication? Don't talk to me about lack of communication."

"I bet you got this at the normal retail price. Can't you ever remember our anniversary in time to send away for something?"

"My wife! My best friend! My second-best friend!"

"*Could I have an au pair bag?*"

". . . and another thing—I want half the wisdom."

"I can't get Joe to make any sort of commitment: He won't even be tied down to coming and going as he pleases."

"And to my wife, Joan,
I leave my mistress,
Valerie."

"Here is a coupon for you good for
one free visit to the shrink."

"We must stop meeting like this—how am
I going to justify you to my accountant?"

"It's ridiculous! Staying together for the sake of the personalized stationery!"

"Deirdre used to whip an egg into it."

"Firstly, gentlemen, has anyone rumbled me and Miss Pettigrew yet?"

"Between you and me, I'm beginning to wonder if she's even a princess."

"My home computer thinks I'm at a conference in Southport."

"My wife understands me—that's why she's having dinner with us."

". . . but that didn't mean you had to launch into a long description of great lulls in the conversations you've known!"

"Come on, Al. You can't fool me. It's time for the floating garden tour and you're going to be on it."

"Another first, Mr Bonington—the South face of Everest in drag."

T. Wood of Brighton, Sussex

1900 CAPTION – HOSTESS. "WHAT DO YOU THINK OF OUR GAME PIE, MR BRIGSON? WE RATHER PRIDE OURSELVES ON IT, YOU KNOW." BRIGSON (NERVOUSLY ANXIOUS TO PLEASE). "OH THANK YOU, IT'S VERY NICE INDEED, WHAT THERE IS OF IT. WHAT I MEAN TO SAY IS, THERE'S PLENTY OF IT – SUCH AS IT IS!" (AWFUL PAUSE!)

"*That was a damn sexist thing to do, Mr Frobisher.*"

"*Could you play something terribly soft-sell?*"

"I'm going to have him for dinner—which wine do you suggest?"

"Rosie thinks I've nipped out for a pint!"

"Maurice and I are planning to attempt something really infra-dig soon."

"My God—I wouldn't like to bump into **him** on a dark night."

"See? Even the wine waiter doesn't understand me."

"It was my fault really. She had nothing to do all day while I was out playing golf."

"Look, when I married you it was the thing to do—now the thing to do is leave you."

"At one time we used to go to all the places he now just sits and plays around with."

"Served him right! It was trying to wall me up that probably
gave him the heart attack."

"Oh, go on—I made the breakfast last year."

"Frankly, Mr Forsyth, I could do this job standing on your head."

"*I notice that when you're talking to yourself you never snarl.*"

"*By the way, do you remember where I put that bottle we were saving for some rather special occasion?*"

"The frustrating thing is I can't
discuss you with my wife."

"He recoiled at something I said, Dr Momfret,
and refuses to come out."

"*Perhaps we're more merchants than adventurers, Mr Harkness.*"

"*That's the fifth bloke she's chucked out for refusing to wipe his feet.*"

"*The unkindest cut of all is that she beats everyone at Bridge.*"

"At least she has the Club nose."

"It just didn't work out. She was a Gemini; I was a Libra. His girlfriend was a Taurus; my boyfriend was a Sagittarius; his wife was a Leo; my common-law husband was a Virgo . . ."

"The kitchens are disgusting, the paintings insanely boring, the staff are on their last legs but the panatellas are delightful."

"*I think they're a marvellous idea.
They tell such dirty stories.*"

"Please, Madam, stop straightening the pictures. We have someone to do that."

"How is it you always manage to get a deep, philosophical point in *your* cracker?"

"Harold, dear—
    I've gone out. Sorry no dinner in the fridge. Dirty dishes
in the sink because dishwasher gone blooey. Cat needs feeding.
Sorry bed is unmade. Vacuum cleaner on the fritz. TV has blown.
Phone dead. Water in basement.

                                        Love, Alice."

"Who's he? He wasn't there this morning."

"I didn't realize going back to your place meant this."
P. Stephens of London, W2

1876 CAPTION – AMENITIES OF THE HONEYMOON. "DON'T MOVE, DARLING! – I'M SO COMFORTABLE, AND YOUR HEAD IS SO SOFT!!"

"It doesn't matter. Nothing I say matters."

"Be quiet, James—I am talking to the floozie. Now then, floozie! Is this your idea of sisterly behaviour?"

"He's loving, attentive, considerate—I believe he's *being **irritated** by another woman.*"

"It's my wedding anniversary. Telephone my husband and tell him you're going to choose me a present."

"Of course you're sexist, that's why you married me!"

"Read? When do I get time to read?"

"Oh, she was a siren once but she's calmed down a lot since then."

*"Remember when I had charisma
and you had a flat?"*

*"Your total indifference as to whether or not I leave has finally
made up my mind. I'm staying."*

"Yes, but do we really **need** crazy paving?"

"I am uncertain how to interpret the dream I had last night—whether it means we can expect seven years of famine, or simply that I may be a repressed homosexual."

"*We live on health foods. My husband is a coward.*"

"Okay, okay—have your say, and I'll re-pack your things for the Hunting Lodge."

"Shall we have one for the wooden hills to Bedfordshire, Miss Brownlow?"

"What do you mean, grounds for divorce? Those are my idiosyncrasies!"

"You realize we'd have nothing to talk about if it weren't for our marriages."

*"We can't win. If you buy this car, **your** wife moves into the spare room . . . if you don't buy this car, **my** wife does!"*

"We have a perfect marriage. Why spoil it by whining for a divorce?"

"I agree that you'd make a perfect husband—but how do I know that divorce mightn't bring out your nasty side?"

"For God's sake, Arlene, couldn't we get our money's worth out of **this** life style **before** we go to the expense of another?"

"The trains are running on time again, darling."

"When are you going to fix that leak outside?"

"Whoever she is she's devoted; I keep finding lipstick on his shoes."

"Sally, I'd like you to meet my soft option."

"The father of the bride and I now pronounce you Vice-President and wife."

"If you don't want to lose your maid, your ox, your ass and everything that is yours—just take your covetous eyes off Sadie Birnbaum!"

"You had better wise up, Albert, there's no room in marriage for someone with a niceness problem!"

"Willie, we've been married for over thirty-five years now. Don't you think it's time we gave some thought to divorce?"

"I've helped keep our marriage alive by baking a little wedding cake every day of our 25 years together."

"Your late husband apologizes for his long silence, and asks you to make allowances for his being dead."

*"I knew he married me for my money—
this is costing me £590."*

*"Strike out 'in
sickness' and
'for poorer'.
It's too
depressing."*

"*I knew you were in a bit of a mess with your VAT, Norman, but I never expected this.*"

"For me?
A key to the executive washroom!"

"I'm sorry, Fiona, but it's the only way
I can tell you how I feel . . ."

"I know, I know! But we're both temporaries in the total scheme of life, Angela."

"I wish I could just press a button and foofh! You and square dancing and bridge and bird watching and cheese fondue would be out of my life forever."

"Goodbye, Arnie, we're leaving you."

"It's Mr Gregory from Accounts."

"Here's to you and me and your husband and my wife."

"Mr Mackley is tied up just now . . ."

"Ah! Canned asparagus spears, like my mother used to open."

"If you but knew how much that implement dates you!"

"*Sid Parker's wife certainly wasn't worth this!*"

"*We started living in sin. Now we live in hell.*"

"*See what I mean? No sense of humour.*"

"It's a small world. Here's one from your third wife and my second husband who are honeymooning in your second wife's first husband's ski chalet."

"You know what I like about you? You don't talk, talk, talk, talk, talk, talk, talk."

"How about a secretary-swapping afternoon?"

"If you'd been a failure, I often wonder how you would have coped with my resentment."

"This ring my husband bought me is the wrong size. I take a five carat."

"... leaving behind the Glue Factory where you wasted seven years in the
Dispatch Department, we now come to the spot where you dallied with Molly
Sudgin which led to your shotgun wedding ..."

"Another day, Harold. Time for you to resume chasing hot deals, rainbows, will-o'-the-wisps and women."